BUSHERS

BUSHERS

BALLPLAYERS DRAWN FROM LEFT FIELD

WRITTEN BY ED ATTANASIO AND
ERIC GOULDSBERRY

ILLUSTRATED BY ED ATTANASIO

 McFarland & Company, Inc., Publishers
Jefferson, North Carolina, and London

ISBN 978-0-7864-7900-9

softcover : acid free paper ∞

LIBRARY OF CONGRESS CATALOGUING DATA ARE AVAILABLE

BRITISH LIBRARY CATALOGUING DATA ARE AVAILABLE

Cover illustrated by Ed Attanasio

Manufactured in the United States of America

*McFarland & Company, Inc., Publishers
Box 611, Jefferson, North Carolina 28640
www.mcfarlandpub.com*

ACKNOWLEDGMENTS

Foremost, I dedicate *Bushers* to my father, who shares my name and passion for the game of baseball. He took me to my first game back in 1967 (at the original Yankee Stadium for a game between the New York Yankees and Minnesota Twins) and coached me during all my Little League years.

Also, I'd like to thank my amazing wife Simone Alexander; the people at the Society for American Baseball Research (SABR); George Krevsky and his staff at the Krevsky Gallery of American Art in San Francisco, because they believed in my art when others said, "What?!"; and finally my writing and baseball partner at thisgreatgame.com, Eric Gouldsberry.—**Ed Attanasio**

TABLE OF CONTENTS

Acknowledgments   v

About the Authors   viii

Introduction   I

Prologue   5

THE PLAYERS   23

ABOUT THE AUTHORS

Ed Attanasio is a freelance advertising and editorial writer, standup comedian and baseball nut. He is a member of SABR (Society for American Baseball Research) and interviews retired ballplayers for its Oral History Committee. He has done more than 100 interviews of retired baseball players since 2000. Ed lives in San Francisco with his wife Simone and his happy dogs.

Eric Gouldsberry is owner of Eric Gouldsberry Art Direction (EGAD), an award-winning graphic design firm operating out of Silicon Valley, California. Eric's creative writing experience goes back to the age of 12, when he wrote sports articles for the local community newspaper. With Ed, Eric co-founded this greatgame.com, the Online Book of Baseball History, in 2005. Eric lives in San Jose with his wife and two children.

INTRODUCTION

I started sketching as a form of rehab after suffering a mini-stroke on August 4, 2009.

The stroke didn't affect my body, but it definitely addled my brain to the point where I was unable to continue my job as a journalist/ad copywriter. My therapists suggested that I should get involved in some type of activity where I'd be using my brain on a daily basis. So, I started drawing a series of illustrations on Post-It-Notes, for hours and hours while I embarked on a slow 14-month recovery.

After drawing one of my characters, I'd hang it up somewhere in the house—on a bathroom mirror, on the wall in the den, even on my dog's forehead. My wife and two stepdaughters always seemed to enjoy these silly illustrations, but eventually they would migrate down to the refrigerator door and, after awhile, they'd disappear. Then, in October of 2011, my wife gave me a notebook and all of the drawings were there—close to 400!

All of these peculiar-looking characters that had emerged from my stroke-scrambled brain were all together and ready for something...but what?

As I browsed through the images, I thought, wow—these illustrations in black felt pen and colored pencils tell a really great story. For more than a year, I didn't know if I would be able to be a professional writer again and these drawings were a map that showed how I recuperated...or maybe digressed, depending on how you look at it!

After I went through all of the images, I found roughly 50 of them depicting imaginary baseball players. I selected 48 of them for my All-Star team and assembled them into a collage entitled "Bushers: A Fantastical Collection of the Craziest Ballplayers You Never Saw."

One day, I decided to submit the collage of the Original '48 Bushers for consideration to appear in an upcoming show at an art gallery in San Francisco. The George Krevsky Gallery of American Art was holding its 15th annual art exhibition called *The Art of Baseball*, and I had visited the show for many years and had written about it, so I was excited about the prospect of Bushers appearing in the exhibit. After a couple of months anxiously waiting for a response from the gallery and not hearing anything I resigned myself to the fact that my sad-sack Bushers might not ever become more than just an amusement for myself, family and friends.

Then, one day the phone rang and the people at the gallery were on the other end. As a writer and a former standup comic, I hate to admit it, but I expect rejection. As the woman on the phone was talking, I was waiting for her next words, telling me that my Bushers were not an ideal match for their show. So, when the people at the Krevsky gallery said they liked the image and wanted to meet me, I was obviously very pleased and surprised. In the end, the collage was accepted into *The Art of Baseball* and it sold before the exhibition began!

So, when my Bushers entered the world, Eric and I decided to use his design skills and the bios we assigned to each player to make an art/humor book featuring my 48 mythical players. Actually, the book contains a total of 50, because we added two bonus babies to make them a nice round number while representing every state in the country. In addition, I then drew a 16-page spread to whimsically describe the Deadball Era, a period in baseball from 1900 to 1919

THE "ORIGINAL 48" BUSHERS COLLAGE BY ED ATTANASIO, WHICH SOLD AT THE GEORGE KREVSKY GALLERY IN SAN FRANCISCO.

when the ball was less lively and, if a player hit 10 home runs, he was considered a power hitter!

We feel it's so unique and entertaining that baseball fans of all ages and even non-fans will enjoy and gravitate toward our crazed players from the mind of a guy who is just lucky to still be alive!

ED ATTANASIO

PROLOGUE

Long before steroids, artificial turf, ice cream dots, luxury boxes, free agency, polyester uniforms and costumed mascots, there was the Deadball Era.

BASEBALL'S DEADBALL YEARS 1900 – 1919

More like a bean bag than a baseball, the Deadball Era's orb
was often used for more than 100 pitches per contest,
back when the spitball was still legal.

The fans of Deadball were a menagerie of gamblers, con men, shady business people and crooked politicians. With ticket prices ranging from two cents to five bucks for the equivalent of today's luxury boxes, anyone and everyone could enjoy this great game.

It was tough for players during the Deadball Era,
well before global warming. The sun was hotter, fleas were
the size of small terriers and mosquitoes as big as ducks.

Early bench jockeying techniques flourished;
colorful retorts and racy remarks were prevalent,
especially between players and umpires.

Unlike today, a career in professional baseball was not considered a respectable job during the Deadball Era. Parents wanted their boys to become doctors, lawyers and teachers, instead of underachievers who were content to play a children's game.

Just like today, morals in the Deadball Era were flexible and
many players accepted money from gamblers to throw
games. Players like Hal Chase, the Eight Black Sox of 1919
and even the legendary Ty Cobb were suspected or
convicted of playing
dirty baseball.

Before political correctness was even a concept, little people,
hunchbacks and disabled people were adopted as mascots
and ball boys. It was a distasteful practice and
was quickly abolished by the 1920s.

Most of the players during the Deadball Era were undereducated. Most were high school or even elementary school dropouts and many were illiterate.

Well before sabermetrics, most Deadball Era players never even knew their batting averages, let alone their on-base percentages, WHIPs or slugging percentages.

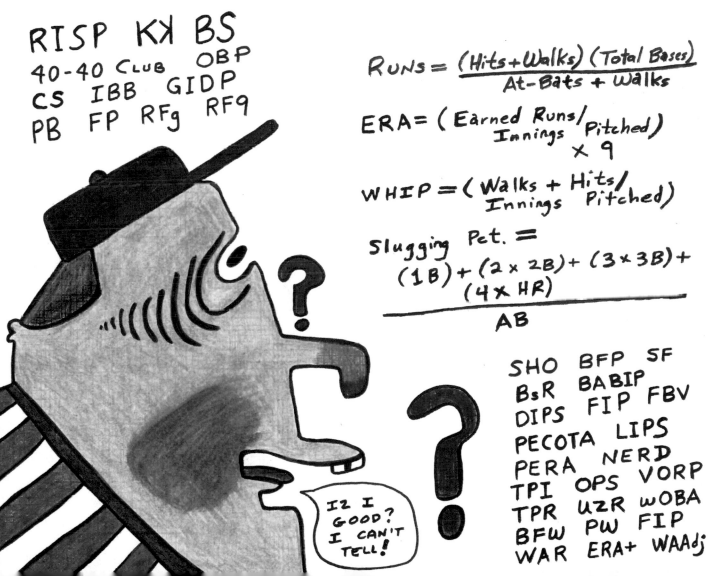

RISP KK BS
40-40 Club OBP
CS IBB GIDP
PB FP RFg RF9

$$RUNS = \frac{(Hits + Walks)(Total\ Bases)}{At\text{-}Bats + Walks}$$

$$ERA = (Earned\ Runs/Innings\ Pitched) \times 9$$

$$WHIP = (Walks + Hits/Innings\ Pitched)$$

$$Slugging\ Pct. = \frac{(1B) + (2 \times 2B) + (3 \times 3B) + (4 \times HR)}{AB}$$

SHO BFP SF
BsR BABIP
DIPS FIP FBV
PECOTA LIPS
PERA NERD
TPI OPS VORP
TPR UZR wOBA
BFW PW FIP
WAR ERA+ WAAdj

IZ I GOOD? I CAN'T TELL!

With a strategy-driven game that relied more on steals
and the hit-and-run, home runs were a rarity.
When John Franklin Baker led the league with 10 in 1912,
they started calling him "Home Run" Baker.

In 1908, a 19-year-old kid named Fred Merkle became the Bill Buckner of
the Deadball Era when he made a tragic baserunning error that cost the
New York Giants a National League pennant against the Chicago Cubs.
Forever known as the "Merkle Boner," it did not deter the first baseman,
who went on to play another fruitful 12 years in the game.

Deadball Era team owners were powerful and therefore were able to underpay players in this pre-union and salary arbitration era. When Mordecai "Three Finger" Brown earned $10,000 in 1914, it was considered an outrageous sum.

Known as the meanest, dirtiest and nastiest player in the history of baseball,
Ty Cobb was hated by his teammates, beat up hecklers and was openly racist.
But, he was one of the greatest players of all time, so much
of his boorish behavior
was ignored.

When Shoeless Joe Jackson took $5,000 to throw the 1919 World Series, Commissioner Kenesaw Mountain Landis kicked him and seven other Chicago White Sox cheaters out of baseball for life. It was hard to believe that Jackson participated in the fix, considering he batted .375 during the series.

As the Deadball Era came to an end, baseball's powers-that-be decided to improve both the baseballs and the bats being used. Bats were limited to 42 inches, but a flat side was still allowed. And when the baseball went to a cork center and was wound more tightly than before, batting averages went up and home runs became more common.

THE PLAYERS

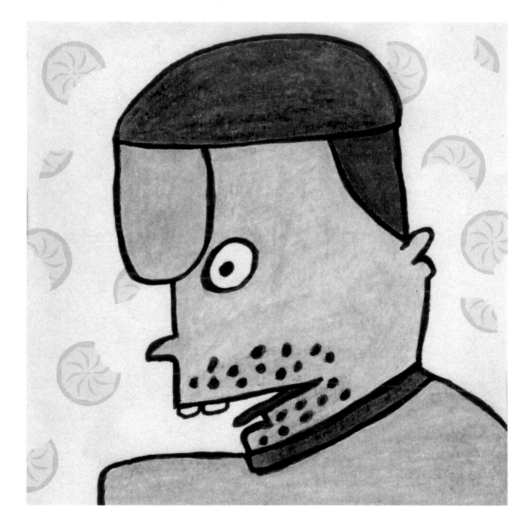

24

COOKIE "CRUMBS" CROZAT

PITCHER

Flea City (California) Larvae
Western Coastal Scrub Brush Association

Crozat loved baseball, but preferred eating cookies on the bench. The crumbs became a problem when birds started flocking toward the dugout. When he was asked to refrain, he could not—and eventually Crozat was sent off to the lowly Will-o-Wisp Wombats, a team of castoffs that played in the Colorado Mite Bowl. Crumbs' baseball career was forgotten, but eventually he found his calling as a baker and launched his very own line of Crumbs' Cookies™.

26

Larry "Low Bridge" Boyle

CATCHER

Briny Beach (Florida) No-see-ems
Sunshine State Association

A former football standout, Boyle was a human obstacle who loved blocking the plate to keep runners from reaching home, whether he had the ball or not. Crouching deeply and refusing to budge, Low Bridge broke noses and bruised egos from Panacea all the way to Yeehaw Junction. After inflecting the need for 16 surgeries, Boyle retired from baseball and started a long, lucrative career as a plastic surgeon, but none of his patients were from the infield.

BENNY "DUCK!" DeCLUE

FIRST BASEMAN
Bucksnort (Texas) Foals
Lone Star League

Because of his large frame and slow-motion maneuvering, DeClue was repeatedly told to "Duck!" during his forgettable 15-year baseball career, but regular collisions with the ball left him bruised, battered and bewildered. Finally after a game versus the Dripping Springs Geysers in which "Duck!" was knocked out by a dripping spitball, the clueless DeClue limped away from the game once and for all.

29

HY "HEAD FIRST" BIZACA

SHORTSTOP
Experiment (Georgia) Egrets
Sweet Peach Federal Association

Bizaca would have had a notable baseball career and memorable, too, for the simple fact that he slid head first into every base, a strategic move intended to unnerve the competition. Unfortunately, Hy jumped head first into everything including relationships, poker games and bar fights. One fatal night while diving recklessly into all three he collided head first into a glass pitcher foisted by Lucy "Unlucky in Love." As a tribute, Head First's baseball buddies buried him by pushing his coffin down a slide and into his final resting place—head first.

Rugger "Barking" Howard

THIRD BASEMAN
Nuttsville (Virginia) Pecans
Carry Me Back League

Rugger was proficient with his hitting and fielding,
but his real talent was dogging opposing teams. He
could rattle players, coaches and umpires with his
verbal catcalls, wolf whistles and his vast repetoire of
authentic dog barks. One afternoon against the Dry
Fork Tines, he was struck in his bespectacled head
by an "errant" pitch. Barking went mad and spent
the remainder of his short life in the Nuttsville
Asylum, barking at the nurses and doctors and
the moon until the lobotomist was notified.

ORSON "STUMBLIN'" URREA

PITCHER
Tingley (Iowa) Gophers
Fields of Opportunity League

Urrea was a solid hitter, but his clumsy running
skills got him into trouble. By trying to stretch
singles into triples, he proudly produced some of
the longest rundowns ever seen in baseball history.
One day during a game against the Beebetown Bees,
Orson fell between second base and third, starting
a rundown that lasted most of the afternoon,
until Stumblin' stumbled all the way home.
Following his baseball days, Stumblin' developed
a speech impediment, but used it to his
advantage when he founded Stumblin' &
Stutterin' Pickles, both dill and sweet.

Eddy "Oft Injured" Amato

OUTFIELDER
Parole (Maryland) Bail Jumpers
Professional East Association

During his short baseball career, Amato's voluminous list of injuries included a sprained eyebrow, a cracked toenail and a severely bruised ego. The ultimate hypochondriac, Eddy sat on his team's disabled list more than he did in the dugout, complaining about every little ache and pain while hitting .122 over three abbreviated, highly agonizing seasons. Oft Injured later became a doctor, but eventually had to retire because all of his patients were contagious.

38

DANTE "CAUGHT STEALING" STAPLETON

THIRD BASEMAN
Quigleyville (Pennsylvania) Quakers
Sammy League

Although Dante couldn't run fast, he was obsessed with base stealing and remained convinced that his very first stolen base was just around the corner. After playing for 12 years and being caught a total of 188 times without a successful swipe, he decided to try literal base stealing, and packed up all four bases in his trunk after a nine-inning game and made a successful run for home. Later, Caught Stealing became a legendary shoplifter, utilizing his base stealing skills in a different field.

40

CLYDE "FIST-FIRST" DENTON

OUTFIELDER

Sweet Lips (Tennessee) Smoochers
Southern Association

Boxing would have been a better sport for Denton, because he preferred punching players over actually hitting baseballs. Used primarily as a pinch runner, "Fist-First" salivated at the opportunity to throw a punch and clocked his opponents at every opportunity. One day, Clyde sucker punched the wrong man—a 300-pound catcher who moonlighted as a bar bouncer and trained for Olympic weightlifting. Finding his fist made no impact, "Fist-First" was forced to bite off a piece of the catcher's ear—which got him permanently pitched from the game.

42

CRAVEN "SWEETS" SIEGEL

SECOND BASEMAN
Antlers (Colorado) Salt Licks
Centennial Mountaineer Federation

Sweets loved his candy and cake and despised long doubleheaders, so as a sweet solution to interminably long afternoons he provided an unending buffet of cotton candy, chocolate bars, licorice, Jolly Ranchers, saltwater taffy and diet soda to his happy (and hyped-up) teammates. Craven ate so much candy he lost all his teeth, contracted diabetes and, at the tender age of 34, retired to the sweet hereafter.

44

Doug "The Rug" Henson

CATCHER

Midnight Thicket (Delaware) Salamanders
Eastern Pioneer League

Henson was known for his slick fielding from behind the plate and the unconvincing hairpiece beneath his cap. During one game against the Dover Sole, The Rug became utterly obsessed with his toupee, which led to a record 23 passed balls that led to seven unearned runs. At one point, The Rug lost his two-dollar wig and called time—but much to his dismay, he discovered that the home plate umpire was using it to sweep off home plate.

46

Buzz "Crooked" Behm

PITCHER
Frogtown (Illinois) Toads
Pipefitters Federal League

Behm had a penchant for cheating rookies during
poker games on long road trips. He led the Toads to
the Big Pipe Series in 1904, but ran into Timmy
"Two Fingers" Alexander, who outpitched and beat
him 2-1 in 23 innings, throwing an astonishing 318
pitches to Behm's 314. Crooked challenged
Alexander to a late night round of poker, but losing
his second game of the day, along with his life
savings, found him to be no rookie.

48

Rocco "Razz" Randazzo

CATCHER
Footville (Wisconsin) Bunions
Dairy Belt League

Randazzo was well known for two things: His colorful bench jockeying techniques and his inability to catch just about anything thrown in his general direction. In 1911, Razz made a tragic mistake when he loudly referred to a pitcher for the Egg Harbor Yolks, Junior "The Bull" Applebaum, as "Bull crap on two legs." As a result, the Bull saw red and slammed Rocco's head into the side of the dugout, at which point Randazzo cut off his tongue and never spoke again. After quitting baseball, he became better known as "Mickey the Mime" and became famous for his signature line of shadow puppets, performed at children's parties and Bar Mitzvahs throughout Wisconsin, from Dyckesville all the way to Spread Eagle.

50

Joe "Tardy" Jones

SECOND BASEMAN
Zap (North Dakota) Zorillas
Lost Careers Conference

Jones was always late and usually entered games
somewhere between the second and third innings,
depending on his activities the night before.
He tried wakeup calls, used four alarm clocks
simultaneously and even hired a gypsy to put him
in a trance so he would never sleep, but nothing
would wake him up. When Tardy passed away in the
late 1920s, the morgue lost his body and so he was
late once again—this time for his own funeral.

52

Floyd "Prancing Fool" Fanucchi

THIRD BASEMAN
Jackpot (Nevada) Jack Rabbits
Tumbleweed Class D League

Fanucchi came from a family of tap dancers,
ballroom competitors and square dancing legends,
so no one was shocked when Floyd started
entertaining fans with his patented moves during
the seventh-inning stretch both at home and on the
road. One particular team—the Pahrump Possums—
was distracted by Fanucchi's dancing, so in the ninth
inning of a close contest, Pahrump's star pitcher Cal
"Close Call" Cavagnaro threw a 100-MPH fastball
that shattered one of the Prancing Fool's kneecaps.
From that day on, he became known as "Gimpy."

54

Freddy "The Flounder" Friedman

OUTFIELDER
Ninety-Six (South Carolina) Bootleggers
Old Coot Class C Federation

Many were convinced that Friedman would be a
star in the majors, but occasional narcolepsy
marred his career. During a 1907 contest against
the Bootleggers' hated rivals, the Caterpillars
of Cuckold's Creek, Freddy had taken a major nap
while trying to stretch a double into a triple.
The Flounder dozed on the infield dirt until he
regained consciousness 12 minutes later. Out of
respect, the Caterpillars' shortstop waited for
Friedman to wake up before tagging him out.

"Slimey" Smead Savage

PITCHER
Monks Hammock (Louisiana) Scallops
Bayou Baseball Federation

Slimey's errant spit-sliders entertained crowds
from Kickapoo to Goober Hill. Savage used
Vaseline, motor oil, butter and even bat guano
to get his ball to dive, rise and shake at the seams.
Most hitters couldn't hit it, but because it was
usually 3-to-4 feet from home plate, they waltzed
around the bases, so pretty soon, Smead was out
of baseball, returning to his family business and
creating a very early version of the Slip 'N Slide.

Morey "Mumbling" Malinosky

SHORTSTOP
Deadhorse (Alaska) Dormice
Class CC Long Nights League

Malinosky loved the frozen fields and long night games under the Alaskan midnight sun, but his teammates tired of his constant and incoherent mumbling. Mumbling would mutter, "I got it!" to claim a ball, but no one could understand, which led to major errors among the infielders.

Consequently, double plays were rare and collisions were commonplace. Malinosky worked with several well-known speech pathologists, but was never able to overcome the mumbling.
In 1912, he was attacked by a large polar bear, scream-mumbling to no avail.

60

Woody "Washout" Woodhull

SHORTSTOP

Elephant Butte (New Mexico) Tuskers
Southwest Drywall League

Woodhull had tryouts with six pro teams, five amateur squads and six church league teams, and he always started out a Hall of Famer. But once the scouting reports were written and opponents pitched to his weaknesses, Woody could never adjust. So he descended in the ranks and eventually failed at every level, earning his unfortunate nickname. In one contest against the Wagon Mound Whompers, Washout struck out six times in a 14-inning game, a record that still stands. Today, whenever another player matches this undistinguished record, it's called "pulling a Woodhull."

62

Pudgy "Pop-Up" Pizzo

FIRST BASEMAN
Looneyville (West Virginia) Loons
Tobacco Harvesters Southern States League

Pizzo was an adept hitter and ran well for his size,
but although he had no trouble fielding even the
toughest groundballs, Pudgy had a phobia that
prevented him from catching routine pop flies.
One day Pizzo claimed that he lost the ball in
the sun—during a heavy hailstorm. In another
game, against the Big Ugly Behemoths,
Pop-Up circled beneath three straight
pop flies, and became so dizzy he had to
be removed from the field on a stretcher.

64

Bernie "The Beak" Bissell

OUTFIELDER

Burnt Water, (Arizona) Mosquitoes
Old Western Settler's League

Bissell's huge nose confused pitchers, because
when he leaned out over home plate, it strongly
resembled a bat. One day while playing against
the Monkey's Eyebrow Howlers, The Beak
accidentally bunted the ball down the third base
line with his prominent snout. Two runs were
scored while umpires and opposing coaches
debated the fairness of using a schnoz for a bat.
Afterward, ice pack in hand, Bernie questioned
God about the fairness of having a
bat for a nose.

Hugh "Hard Mitt" Henderson

SHORTSTOP
Walla Walla (Washington) Sweet Onions
Evergreen State League

Henderson could hit for power and average, but his fielding was atrocious. In one contest versus the Tumtum Tumblers in 1901, Hard Mitt booted four grounders, dropped two pop-ups and threw six balls in the stands—all in two-thirds of an inning. Consequently, he was sent off to the low, low sandlot leagues, where he fell victim to quicksand.

Vern "Stinky" Schembri

Schembri was a marvelous player, but his
teammates could not tolerate his funky body
odor. With a diet consisting of beans, cabbage
and bleu cheese, Vern was always gassy and
could be counted on to clear out the clubhouse.
One day in 1913, Stinky caused two umpires,
three spectators and a batboy to pass out by
producing a cloud of flatulence. It hung
over the ballpark for three days,
causing the Beavers to forfeit two games,
as the competitors cried, "foul!"

Preston "The Preacher" Piercy

PITCHER
Whynot (North Carolina) Wood Frogs
Piedmont Triad Federation

Piercy was a fundamentalist preacher who never
grasped the fundamentals of baseball. He called
the pitching mound "my pulpit," and with a
career batting average at .012, Preston called
the batter's box "my purgatory," and the dugout
"my own private inferno." In a game against
the Lizard Lick Skinks in 1904, The Preacher
allowed 14 runs on 21 hits and 11 walks in just
five innings, but in the process converted
12 opposing players to his faith:

Can I get an Amen!

72

Hap "Snoozing" Stiles

SECOND BASEMAN
Gobblers Crossing (Alabama) Drumsticks
Sweet Home League

When he wasn't sleeping on the bench, Stiles was fighting with his twin brothers who doubled as teammates: Harold "The Nightmare" and Harlin "The Big Snore" Stiles. With their sister and bat girl Apnea on the bench, this quartet slept, tossed and turned in every small town from Coal Fire to Cluttsville. A talented hitter, Stiles once homered— stretching his arms around first, yawning as he crossed second, and nodding off around third. After retiring from the great game he slept through, Stiles and his siblings became permanent participants in a sleep research study.

74

Ruben "Rabbit Ears" Romero

CATCHER
Seed Tick (Arkansas) Suckers
Land of Opportunity League

Physically speaking, Romero was a solid, strong catcher. But his highly sensitive, thin-skinned nature, and long, pointy ears made him a prime target for bench jockeys from Turkey Scratch to Goobertown. One day, several opposing players rode Rabbit Ears so hard that he fled the ballpark in a torrent of tears. After his retirement from baseball, Ruben became a very successful psychologist—with his rabbit-like ears, turns out he was a great listener!

76

Bryce "The Burglar" Bednarz

OUTFIELDER
Muddy Gap (Wyoming) Moose
Forever West Federation

Bednarz was slow-footed in the field, but his side
job as a house burglar flourished for several decades.
In close games on the road, The Burglar would
fake an injury so that he could leave the game,
sneak out of the clubhouse and break into
homes from Big Hole to Pumpkin Buttes.
One evening, he broke into the wrong house
and found himself on the business side of
a double barrel shotgun. An hour later,
he was returned to the ballpark tied up, naked
as a jaybird and blushing like a bride.

78

Seymour "Sow Caller" Reynolds

SECOND BASEMAN
Lame Deer (Montana) Salt Licks
Drywall Hangers League

Seymour was raised on a farm where the pigs
idolized him and vice versa. He couldn't run,
hit or field, but on occasion he would make a
spectacular error and thrill the crowd, with
a fantastically foul stream of pork-laced invective.
Sow Caller played for six teams in just two years,
and then became a star pig caller on the vaudeville
circuit throughout the Northwest. *Suey!*

ELMER "WILD WILD" WICKS

CATCHER
Comical Corners (New Jersey) Wiseguys
Jerry Eastern League

Wild Wild Wicks set an all-time season record
that will never be matched: 54 passed balls, two
passed kidney stones and 13 catcher interference calls.
Wicks dreamed of rainouts and those rare balls
that actually found their way into his porous glove.
In 1911, he retired from baseball and was
recruited to join the Mafia, until he dropped
some betting slips and ended up residing
in the Jersey River with a brand new
set of concrete shoes.

82

Vern "Wrong Turn" Weimers

OUTFIELDER
Dent Ford (Missouri) Moles
Show-Me Association

Weimers' base running snafus are legendary. One day while playing against the Joplin Jellyfish, old Wrong Turn decided to go directly to second base on a single to right. The Jellyfish pitcher was startled as he approached the mound, so the hurler leg-whipped Vern and a fight ensued. Another time, Wrong Turn skipped second base completely and ran a straight line to third from first after launching a shot against the center field wall in a game against the Neck City Cricks. Weimers could never figure out the baserunning basics of baseball; years later, all was explained when he became the first person to be diagnosed with a rare condition, known as diamond dyslexia.

84

LAMAR "LIPS" LENHART

PITCHER
Suckerville (Maine) Lampreys
Northeast Senior Circuit

Lenhart had a decent curveball, a bad attitude and a set of lips that could "sink ships" according to legendary sportswriter Pens Elliott. One afternoon while throwing a shutout against the Beans Corner Bingo Pintos, Lamar's enormous lips took on a life of their own. With a pitch in mid-air and racing toward the Pintos' top hitter, Lenhart's irrepressible lips slurped and smacked the hitter's face in what could only be interpretted as a kiss. Lips finished the shutout by easily striking out the remaining Pintos' players, petrified and confused by what is today known as the infamous "Smack heard 'round the world."

Miles "Addy" Baddeson

OUTFIELDER
Neversink (New York) Ramblers
East Coast Federation

Baddeson was afflicted with ADD (Attention Deficit Disorder) long before anyone knew what it was. His manager and fans thought he was easily distracted, but a decent player nonetheless. In one game against the Fishkill Filets, Miles was beaned when an easy fly ball skulled him, opening a huge gash in his forehead. When they asked what happened, Baddeson explained that he was reading advertisements emblazoned along the outfield fence. His skipper began calling him Addy that day. Baddeson went on to become one of the great ad copywriters of all time, composing copy while fielding fly balls.

Stan "The Gland" Bullard

PITCHER

Mosquitoville (Vermont) Larvae
Maple Syrup Association

They say success requires 110% perspiration, but in Bullard's case it was more like 200%. After getting cut by the Notown Trappers for being "soggy," The Gland ended up in Mosquitoville, a town known for excellent peanut brittle and serious bug bites. Stan went 7-0 on the road but was winless at home, tortured by the town's hummingbird-size sweat-enamored mosquitoes.

90

Milo "Groundout" Gurries

THIRD BASEMAN
Woonsocket (Rhode Island) Quahogs
Red Hen Circuit Association

Gurries hit the ball hard every time—but straight
down into the ground. As opposed to dribblers
and weak rollers, Groundout's sharply hit mole
chasers were tailor-made for easy double plays.
In one game, he set a record by grounding
six double killers and one triple play. His
teammates had seen enough and sent him
on the next train to the Block Island Mortar
Heads, a class DD League squad consisting
of castoffs from other teams.

92

Freddy "The Forehead" Friday

OUTFIELDER
Smileyberg (Kansas) Grins
Corn Syrup Federation

Furrowed and large, Friday's enormous forehead was immediately recognizable by fans and favored as a target for opposing pitchers. With a head described as "80 percent forehead and 20% face," Freddy was mocked by teams from Skiddy to Agenda. But in a bench-clearing brawl during a game against the Buttermilk Guernseys, The Forehead simultaneously head-butted three opponents— knocking each one out cold. Freddy gained great respect that day, at least until the local police showed up and arrested him for assault with a deadly weapon.

94

Sully "Slo Mo" Durbin

FIRST BASEMAN
Hot Coffee (Mississippi) Scalders
Bayou States League

While the rest of the world operated on real time,
Durbin ran the race of life a half step slower. Fans
laughed as he slowly chugged around the bases,
turning triples into singles. His coaches "clocked
him with a sun dial," they claimed. With the reflexes
of a snail, the sloth-like Slo Mo led the Scalders in
grounding into double plays and was hit by more
errant pitches than any other player in the sketchy
history of the Bayou States League.

Buzz "The Brain" Berghammer

SECOND BASEMAN
Belchertown (Massachusetts) Chuggers
Baked Beans Eastport League

They said Buzz had an abacus in his head and a library in his brain. By quickly calculating opposing players' statistics, using his photographic memory and 145 IQ, The Brain assisted his pitchers by providing them with the useful stats. Unfortunately, the light-hitting second baseman could never outhit his IQ, so he spent most of his time on the bench—with a pencil in hand and deep into performance analysis. He is now considered to be among the founding fathers of Sabremetrics.

ELMO "LIMBURGER FEET" WATSON

OUTFIELDER

Nimrod (Minnesota) Flying Crows
10,000 Lakes League

His feet smelled like cheese and his performance
stunk up the field, but Elmo Watson was a beloved
player for one main reason—the other team
could not handle his cheesy feet. The Flying
Crows used Limburger Feet to their advantage
whenever they could—strategically positioning
him downwind at crucial times.

CLARENCE "SIX FINGERS" FISCHER

PITCHER
Eden (Michigan) Muskrats
Big Mitt League

We all remember Mordecai "Three Finger" Brown, and many recall "Thumbs" Curry, but few know the legend of ol' Six Fingers, born with an extra digit on his right hand. The kids at school relentlessly teased little Clarence, but the additional finger allowed Clarence to grip a baseball in such a way that it flew out of his hand with an unusual spin on it. When he finally hit the bush leagues, opposing teams protested that the extra finger gave him an unfair advantage. The argument always failed, because as one writer said, "If he was born with two heads, we'd still let him play, so what's the big deal with one extra finger?"

"Semi-Marvelous" Marville Munno

Outfielder
Knockemstiff (Ohio) Ogres
Old Rookie League

Munno was renowned for playing well—about half the time. When Semi-Marvelous wasn't showboating, he hit like an All-Star, stole bases and threw out runners right and left. But when he was off his game, Munno looked like a blind cat trying to catch a sparrow. His inconsistency was perfectly illustrated during a doubleheader against the Businessberg Bluesuits. In the first contest, Marville hit for the cycle and stole three bases while playing a spectacular left field. In the nightcap, he stumbled and bumbled, committing three errors in one inning and striking out four times. Semi-Marvelous retired after a 12-year career full of ups and downs, moving on to a series of semi-successful business ventures.

104

MICKEY "CEMENT HEAD" MAGEE

OUTFIELDER
Bowlegs (Oklahoma) Shufflers
Horizon Association

Legendary players in baseball history used their
unique skills to excel at this great game. But, in
the case of Magee, with his rare compulsion to
head-butt baseballs, fans, outfield walls, umpires,
opposing players—even his own teammates—it
kept him forever playing at the lowest depths
of the bush leagues, where he eventually
learned to keep his head to himself.

BILLY "BAD ANSWER" BAKER

RELIEF PITCHER
Roach (Nebraska) Ramblers
Tornado Semi-Pro Circuit

Baker was a sneaky relief pitcher decades before
most teams used them. With a wicked curve, a
sizzling slider and a spitball that ran away from
hitters like a scared cat, Billy was adept on the
mound—but graceless when dealing with reporters.
Once, when asked how to spell relief, Bad Answer
cocked an eyebrow, cocked his leg and replied,
"This is how I spell relief," while relieving
himself on the unamused reporter's shoe.

108

Rudy "No Curfew" Schenkel

PITCHER
Giants Neck (Connecticut) Clam Bakes
Old Greenwich League

Schenkel partied more than he pitched and, in
the end, he drank himself into political office.
Known for late nights chasing young nubile
female groupies, No Curfew was repeatedly fined
for not returning to the team hotel or train in
towns from Havemayer Park all the way to Mystic.
When elected to Connecticut Congress in 1914,
it was much easier to justify his frequent
absenses by explaining that he had
been out hiking.

Wilbur "The Wind" Winchell

SECOND BASEMAN

Sandwich Landing (New Hampshire) Hoagies
Crop Dusters Federation

The Wind loved cabbage and red beans for breakfast.
A sharp fielding, light-hitting middle infielder,
Winchell regularly sickened his opponents,
especially during double plays. With adept timing
and total control, The Wind could express
himself at the most opportune times, once
gassing out half a dozen members of the
Hell Hollow Hedonists on a blistering hot
Saturday afternoon. Opponents prayed that Mother
Nature's wind would blow in and towards the
Hoagies' dugout when The Wind was in the lineup.

Marshall "The Mouth" McIntyre

THIRD BASEMAN
Papa'i (Hawaii) Poi
Pacific Island Association

A skilled bench jockey, McIntyre riled up Hawaii's best players from Cod Fish Village all the way to Pepeekeo with his humorous tirades and pinpoint needling. The Mouth was especially adept at razzing opponents in six languages and more than two dozen dialects. During one game against the Pearl City Necklaces, Marshall harassed two umpires, six opposing players, one batboy and a handful of local drunks, but fortunately, since no one could understand him, nobody took offense.

Gene "Mr. Nice" Nunes

PITCHER
Mud Butte (South Dakota) Dusters
Great Frontier Conference

Leo Durocher famously once said, "Nice guys finish last," but Nunes was a cultured gentleman who respected and honored the competition. He never cursed an umpire, never spiked an opponent and always bowed to the ladies in the stands. Unfortunately, he had a rubber arm and threw fat slow pitches that were no mystery to opposing hitters. While Mr. Nice was polite to everyone he encountered, the league gave him a rude goodbye after a 1-14 record. His lone win came when the opposing Buffalo Gap Dungchasers threw the game because they felt they owed it to him for so many years of unmatched courteousness.

Eddy "The Edifice" Edwards

CATCHER

Loafers Station (Indiana) Loiterers
Old Hoosiers League

Runners could not run through Edwards on their
way to the plate, and since he was a solid six feet tall
weighing in at 265 pounds, they could not navigate
around him either. During one contest against the
feared Sligo Slugs, Edwards blocked the plate while
Billy "The Behemoth" Barron ran The Edifice
down, breaking his collarbone and knocking out
more than a few teeth. As a result, Eddy retired
on the spot and entered the construction field,
ironically building edifices from Needmore
all the way to Steam Corner.

BURTON "BUNIONS" BUNN

OUTFIELDER
Mexican Hat (Utah) Sombreros
Razor Peaks Federation

Burton had a powerful bat and a slick glove, but Paul
Bunyan–sized bunions on both feet caused him to
stumble and trip around the bases throughout the
lower leagues of Utah for more than a decade.
Size 14 shoes didn't make things any easier for
old Bunions, but at least he could commiserate
with his teammate, Hank "Hangnail" Hardin.

Hy "Hit and Run" Dunne

SECOND BASEMAN
Priest River (Idaho) Kneelers
Mountain Bluebird Division

In the age of the dead ball, Dunne was exceptional at the hit-and-run. Alas, he was also a veteran of numerous hit-and-run accidents outside the lines—usually as a result of rushing to the ballpark in his Ford Model T at the very last minute. Dunne's bad habit wasn't restricted to home games; on the road at Beer Bottle Crossing one afternoon, Hit-and-Run kept everyone waiting at the hotel as the game approached. Once they finally boarded the trolley, they discovered that the driver was asleep. Dunne immediately took control of the situation and commandeered the trolley—running down a fruit cart, an old wagon and a police trolley—before continuing on to the ballpark without pause.

LARRY "LADIES' DAY" LANDIS

PITCHER
Sunfish (Kentucky) Waders
Goldenrod Association

A highly skilled flirt with an infatuation with the ladies in the stands, Landis always lost his focus on the batters—leading to innumerable errant pitches directed at the girls who caught his gaze, causing them to disperse like frightened geese. No one dared sit anywhere near the attractive female fans, for fear of getting hit. As a result, opposing teams from Possum Trot to Bugtussle always held their annual Ladies' Day when Larry came to town and, somewhat surprisingly, all the local ladies were willing to take one for the team.

McFarland Graphic Novels

Yellow Rose of Texas: The Myth of Emily Morgan.
Written by Douglas Brode; Illustrated by Joe Orsak. 2010

Horrors: Great Stories of Fear and Their Creators.
Written by Rocky Wood; Illustrated by Glenn Chadbourne. 2010

Hutch: Baseball's Fred Hutchinson and a Legacy of Courage.
Written by Mike Shannon; Illustrated by Scott Hannig. 2011

*Hit by Pitch: Ray Chapman, Carl Mays and
the Fatal Fastball.* Molly Lawless. 2012

*Werewolves of Wisconsin and Other American Myths,
Monsters and Ghosts.* Andy Fish. 2012

Witch Hunts: A Graphic History of the Burning Times.
Written by Rocky Wood and Lisa Morton;
Illustrated by Greg Chapman. 2012

*Hardball Legends and Journeymen and Short-Timers: 333
Illustrated Baseball Biographies.* Ronnie Joyner. 2012

The Accidental Candidate: The Rise and Fall of Alvin Greene.
Written by Corey Hutchins and David Axe; Art by Blue Delliquanti. 2012

Virgin Vampires: Or, Once Upon a Time in Transylvania.
Written by Douglas Brode; Illustrated by Joe Orsak. 2012

Great Zombies in History.
Edited by Joe Sergi. 2013

Bonnie & Clyde — The Beginning.
Written and drawn by Gary Jeffrey. 2013